Anna Sim
(757) 229-7882

Depression Era Dime Store Glass

C.L. Miller

Schiffer Publishing Ltd

4880 Lower Valley Road, Atglen, PA 19310

Published by Schiffer Publishing Ltd.
4880 Lower Valley Road
Atglen, PA 19310
Phone: (610) 593-1777; Fax: (610) 593-2002
E-mail: Schifferbk@aol.com
Please visit our web site catalog at
www.schifferbooks.com

This book may be purchased from the publisher.
Include $3.95 for shipping.
Please try your bookstore first.

We are interested in hearing from authors
with book ideas on related subjects.

You may write for a free catalog.

In Europe, Schiffer books are distributed by
Bushwood Books
6 Marksbury Rd.
Kew Gardens
Surrey TW9 4JF England
Phone: 44 (0)181 392-8585; Fax: 44 (0)181 392-9876
E-mail: Bushwd@aol.com

Copyright © 1999 by C. L. Miller
Library of Congress Catalog Card Number: 98-83141

All rights reserved. No part of this work may be reproduced or used in any form or by any means—graphic, electronic, or mechanical, including photocopying or information storage and retrieval systems—without written permission from the copyright holder.
"Schiffer," "Schiffer Publishing Ltd. & Design," and the "Design of pen and ink well" are registered trademarks of Schiffer Publishing Ltd.

Book Designed by Randy L. Hensley
Type set in American XBd BT/Souvenir Lt BT

ISBN: 0-7643-0665-0
Printed in China
1234

Contents

Dedication

To Dorothy Sollars Daughtery (1897-1960), who touched countless lives in beautiful ways and inspired all to fulfill their dreams.

Dorothy Sollars Daughtery.

Acknowledgments

My appreciation to each of the following for their support and contributions during the development of this publication. If I have overlooked anyone, I apologize at this time. Daniel W. Andrews, Rod and Sally Blackstone, Neal and Patti Byerly, Cambria County Library System of Johnstown, Pennsylvania, Russ and Donna Colwell, Julie Collart, Columbus Public Library of Columbus, Ohio. James L. Cooper, Ann C. Davis, Detroit Public Library of Detroit, Michigan, Douglas B. Dupler, Ela Area Public Library of Lake Zurich, Illinois, Ela Historical Society of Lake Zurich, Illinois, Mrs. Walter Evans, Karen L. Evans, Sadie B. Evans, Larry Flinchpaugh, Carolyn K. Frash, Carolyn Haas, Mary Ann Heft, Bill Hicks, Hoopeston Public Library of Hoopeston, Illinois, Ida Public Library of Belvidere, Illinois, Larry and Karen Kanter, Ronald E. Keister, Lon and Lynda Lemons, Lynn Public Library of Lynn, Massachusetts, Casey and Chris McGowan, Jacqulyn Diane Miller, Ralph and Linda Miller, Joan E. Neel, Merry Palicz, Carl and Bonnie Riddlebarger, Byron Rider, Rochester Public Library (Local History Division) of Rochester, New York, Mike and Cindy Schneider, Suzanne Studer, The Cherubs Chest Awesome Antiques-Royal Oak, Michigan, Todd Turner, Barbara G. Vanchieri, Steve P. and Jackie J. Wolfe, Stephanie J. Wolfe and Nancy J. Weller.

To Lisa M. Gonzales for her friendship, support and her invaluable assistance in acquiring documents for this publication.

Foreword

This book is designed to aid collectors in recognizing glassware and/or related merchandise that was available or associated with any five-and-ten-cent store, whether it was Ben Franklin, H.L. Green, W.T. Grant's, S.S. Kresge, S.H. Kress, McCrory, McLellan, G.C. Murphy, J.J. Newberry, Neisner's, Lamston, Schultz's Bros., or F.W. Woolworth's.

These stores were once a staple item along "Main Street, U.S.A." The china, glassware, and various merchandise they carried has become highly collectible and is escalating in both price and demand. Many patterns of glassware were reserved for exclusive sale through one or another of the stores listed above; these patterns were available in any quantity or could be purchased in complete sets.

It is impossible to provide extensive historical information or a complete listing, in either photographs or documentation, of every pattern of glassware that was sold from the bins and counters of the dime stores. I have provided information available from my own records and those made possible through other sources. If I have made mistakes or mislead anyone, I apologize at this time.

Some time ago, I retrieved an original 1939-1943 wholesale distribution catalogue from an old storage trunk at a local flea market. It listed various merchandise that was available to many of the five-and ten-cent stores, and many of those original documents and/or photographs appear throughout this publication. The original text from this catalogue provided captions, dates, and retail prices. Without those records this project could never have been undertaken.

Whether you are a novice or already a serious collector of glassware, I hope you enjoy this publication and I invite you to examine and enjoy the counters of the five-and-ten-cent stores.

Postcard showing McCrory's and Woolworth's located side by side on Cleveland Street, Clearwater, Florida. $4-$6.

Introduction

This book was created as I sat in the luncheonette section of America's most famous five-and-ten-cent store, the F.W. Woolworth Co., In Columbus, Ohio. This 118-year-old American icon with its scarlet and gold trademark was still operating four hundred stores in most major cities across the United States at the time I first began this writing in 1996.

On that winter morning, I gathered together my notebook, pen, twenty dimes, fifteen nickels, and additional cash—just in case—and boarded a city bus close to my home. I rode downtown, where I was able to get off at a bus stop just steps away from Woolworth's front door. This store has thrived along a primary street in Columbus since 1937.

Woolworth's famous trademark first appeared in Columbus when the F.M. Kirby & Co., a Pennsylvania corporation of ninety-six stores and sales of $7,253,036, merged with Woolworth in 1912. By 1919, F.W. Woolworth was operating two Columbus stores: one was listed at 105-111 North High Street and the second was located at 220-222 East Main Street. Both of these early stores have since closed.

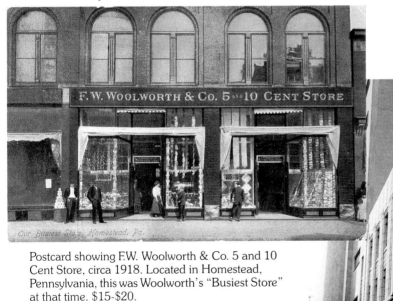

Postcard showing F.W. Woolworth & Co. 5 and 10 Cent Store, circa 1918. Located in Homestead, Pennsylvania, this was Woolworth's "Busiest Store" at that time. $15-$20.

The F.W. Woolworth Co. in Columbus, Ohio, where the Introduction to this book was created. This store originally opened in 1937.

Breakfast in Woolworth's

Inside the Woolworth store, I seated myself in a booth at the end of the long counter that provided a view of the surrounding activities and operations of the store. From the menu located in a chrome holder attached to the booth, I placed my order. No. 1—two eggs with bacon or sausage, hash browns, and toast with jelly—was priced at $2.95; a cup of coffee was an additional .85 with free refills.

In quality, quantity, and price, a plate luncheon, sandwich, or soda purchased at the luncheonette in one Woolworth store was identical to the same item in any other Woolworth's. Menus did vary, to conform to local tastes and location of the store.

Woolworth menu, ca. 1997. $10-$12.

The luncheonette section of the F.W. Woolworth Co. in Columbus, Ohio. Woolworth's was America's most famous five-and-ten-cent store.

After taking my order, the waitress moved back to the front counter, which was occupied by a diverse clientele including senior citizens, business executives in fashionable suits, blue-collar workers in flannel shirts and jeans, young housewives with children bundled up against the morning cold, teen-agers, and African-Americans, all seated on revolving red padded stools. Across from the counter the grill cook continued to fill orders left by the waitress.

For many years, African-Americans were denied access to many Woolworth lunch counters. Then in 1960, four young black students were denied lunch at the Woolworth counter in Greensboro, North Carolina, setting off a fifty-city protest that forced Woolworth to change its discriminatory practices. This event launched the American civil rights movement. The counter from the Greensboro store was moved and is now displayed in the Smithsonian's Museum of American History.

Woolworth was not the only store to deny access to black individuals. In 1929, for example, the S.H. Kress Five-and-Ten-Cent Store in Montgomery, Alabama, had two completely separate entrances. The Dexter Avenue entrance was for the whites, the other entrance on Monroe Street was for the black trade. The company aimed its business at both groups, but only whites were allowed to eat at the lunch counter. In the 1940s, a take out counter marked "Colored Only" was located near the Monroe Street entrance. Two identical marble water fountains were built into a wall side by side against a marble back splash. Carved overhead one was the word "Colored" while the other indicated "White."

On that morning in 1996, however, I saw no signs of discrimination or distinguishing differences.

After a hardy breakfast, I took my bill to a cash register located midway between the counter and the booths. Gone now were the nickels and dimes that had jingled in my pocket, as well as some of my additional cash—all needed to cover the bill and a tip left at the booth.

Shopping at Woolworth's

Thoughout the store was a series of aisles running the length of the store in all four directions, a center open stairwell directing shoppers to the lower level, and a back stairwell advising shoppers to check the level below.

On the main floor, various shelves were filled with a considerable amount of precisely arranged merchandise. Across the front section, between two main entrance doors, was located the check out counter, where salesgirls wearing Woolworth smocks calculated purchases on an electric cash register.

As I made my way down the aisles, I noticed that the broad range of merchandise and the corresponding prices were no longer within the range of a nickel and a dime, which I had already spent and more in the luncheonette anyway. Those days were long gone.

Above the open center stairwell and escalator hung a sign indicating that on the "Lower Sales Floor" was an array of "Art Goods, Pillows, Hardware, Housewares, China, Home Furnishings, Curtains, Drapes, Lamps, Paint, Pets, Horticulture, Furniture, Shades, Yard Goods, Patterns, Toys, Books and Wearing Apparel." I descended down the escalator, still in search of the ultimate 5¢ or 10¢ article. It was all "self-service" now; should I need assistance a sign and a bell were provided for me to ring. By the time I left the store, the additional cash in my wallet had come in handy and my purchases totaled $27.85, much more than the nickel or dime I had originally hoped to spend.

If Woolworth customers needed assistance in making a selection, they could ring a bell that was provided near a sign such as this one (original bell missing). The sign was held in place by a metal "T" stand. Sign $5-$10. Bell $10-$15.

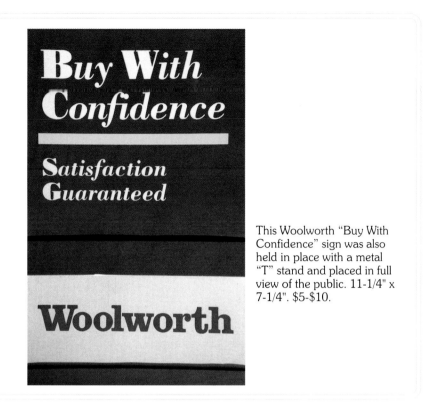

This Woolworth "Buy With Confidence" sign was also held in place with a metal "T" stand and placed in full view of the public. 11-1/4" x 7-1/4". $5-$10.

A Reputation Was Made

In 1880, the five-and-ten-cent stores had a reputation as being the poor person's department store. After World War I and during the early 1920s, dime stores experienced extraordinary success and became an American institution. During the Depression of the 1930s, nickels and dimes were still being spent at the local five-and-ten-cent stores. At Kresge's, the policy of "Nothing Over 10 Cents In Store" prevailed until World War I, when inflation finally forced prices up.

Buying Habits

In 1925, the type of goods found in retail stores could be divided into three types: (1) convenience goods, which were goods customarily purchased at easily accessible stores for nominal prices; (2) shopping goods, defined as those for which the consumer desired to compare price, quality, and style; and (3) specialty goods, which were those that had some particular appeal other than price, making customers willing to visit the store in which the item was sold, no matter where it was located.

"F.W. Woolworth Co." register No. 1 money bag. $8-$12.

A selection of "Ohio Sales Tax" official prepaid tax cards and "Prepaid Sales Tax" consumer's receipts (stamps). Cards were good in only those stores indicated on each card. Vendors stamped on the above cards were: J.J. Newberry Co., Morris 5¢ and 10¢ Stores, and F.W. Woolworth Co. On the front of each card appeared: "The vendor must in the presence of the customer indicate the amount of the taxable sale by punching the exact amount of every sale in every instance at the time the transaction is made. Willful violation of any provision of this act with respect to the use of such cards shall subject vendor to revocation of license." *Davis Collection.* $20-$25 complete selection.

Stores associated with convenience goods were often located at points most easily reached by the consumer, while shopping goods stores were centrally located in a retail district and drew trade from a wide area. The locations of specialty goods stores were often accessible, but in many cases not. Location played a tremendous part in the volume of business the stores were able to produce. It was estimated that between 75 to 95 percent of the business was with women, and a location distasteful to women hindered sales. Often stores opened across from or next to other existing establishments.

Postcard showing Kresge's and Woolworth's on Kansas Avenue, Topeka, Kansas. Stores often benefited from the traffic of their competitors by locating near each other. $2-$4.

Three features were important in acquiring a good location. The first was proximity to other businesses, because the virtues of the location would be shed upon the location of the store. Proximity to a pool room, barber shop, or places were men congregated, for example, detracted from the value of a location. The second important feature was nearness to places where crowds assembled on busy days; this meant shopping convenience and was a plus for incidental sales. Finally, the principal path of traffic could interfere with business if not wisely selected.

In many stores, December sales amounted to 25 percent of the stores' annual business. Most stores divided all seasonal goods into two classes: merchandise sold only in certain seasons due to climatic or seasonal conditions, and merchandise such as toys and novelties sold through impulse buying for special holidays or in the spirit of some tradition. After Christmas came Valentine's Day, Easter, Fourth of July, and Halloween merchandise. In some cities, St. Patrick's Day provided a good selling opportunity as well.

Store managers were often instructed to learn the trends of their customers' wants and needs, anticipate them, and try to find some needs which they could meet with merchandise the consumer might have neglected to purchase. The sale of such goods meant profit and excellent service to the trade; another advantage was that it provided opportunities to sell specialties that would draw attention to a store, bringing in people looking for items with specific requirements.

The large amount of inexpensive stock displayed throughout the store was acquired from various distributors and/or from the manufacturer, allowing it to be sold at low prices. One such supplier was "Butler Brothers," who sold the first assortment of small nickel and dime merchandise to the earliest stores. Their first sale amounted to $800. In 1925, Butler Brothers had locations in New York, Chicago, St. Louis, Minneapolis, and Dallas. They published various manuals on "Storekeeping" and "How To Take Inventory," as well as an assortment of "Bookkeeping and Store Control" publications and business forms. It is impossible to provide a complete listing of the large scale wholesale distributors often referred to as the "Jobber."

Hiring the Right Salesgirl

In 1925, some variety stores refused to employ older women. They believed older women were too difficult to train and not accepting of new ideas. Many stores refused to employ sisters, because experience had taught them that when a conflict between sisters took place it often cost the store money. There were also merchants who would not employ girls who had worked in "high class" city stores; the merchants believed they were inclined to ignore the small town girls.

The best type of "Salesgirls" were girls who lived at home and were not altogether dependent on employment for their financial existence. They were intelligent and anxious to learn what they could in order to develop into good employees. Some of the best "Salesgirls" were inexperienced town girls who worked for the first time in a variety store. Experienced or inexperienced, salesgirls had to be honest.

In 1918, Woolworth employed more than 35,000 regular employees, most of whom were girls and 1,536 of whom had five years of service. When a Woolworth "Salesgirl" with three years or more of service left the company to get married, she received a substantial cash wedding present.

Many five-and-ten-cent stores required their "Salesgirls" and/or luncheonette staff to wear uniforms. All S.H. Kress "Salesgirls," for example, wore tan uniforms trimmed in brown. Many stores provided smocks as well as name tags that could be attached to one's clothing as a means of identification. These simple identification tags with any dime store trademark are collectible. On the secondary market they bring anywhere from $5.00 to $25.00, depending on the condition and the rarity of the tag. Similarly, vintage uniforms from any dime store are sought by many clothing collectors. Prices vary from $10.00 to $50.00 for complete vintage or period uniforms in excellent condition.

Store Rules

A list of store rules was often posted or given to every girl. The following "Rules," taken from Butler Brothers' "Manual of Variety Storekeeping," © 1925, were popular during that year:

1. "These RULES are furnished you for the purpose of acquainting you with the policy of this store and for your information as to what is required of all employees."

2. "Failure to observe the rules will meet with instant dismissal. It is our policy to keep in our employ only those who require the fewest reminders of infractions of the rules."

3. "Always arrive on time—never late—and return from your meals within an hour."

4. "Inform your friends and relatives not to call you on the telephone or visit you in the store—except in absolutely necessary cases—then to make it very brief."

5. "No clerk will be retained who has visitors coming to this store to see her. Therefore, it is to your interest to inform them promptly of this RULE."

6. "Goods will be sold at a discount to employees. They must make all purchases from the manager after closing hours or when off duty."

7. "All parcels, bundles, lunches, parasols, coats, hats, purses and money belonging to sales ladies must always be left in the office upon arrival at the store, and remain there until leaving the store. LET IT BE THOROUGHLY UNDERSTOOD THAT NO MONEY IS TO BE ON THE PERSON OR IN THE PERSONAL POSSESSION OF ANY CLERK WHILE ON DUTY."

8. "Do not leave the store without permission of the manager. Do not EAT or CHEW GUM while on duty. Clerks will be given permission to leave the store at any time they request it, but do not ask except when necessary."

9. "Always ring sales immediately in the nearest register. Do not stand, work or sell goods from the aisles except when necessary. Work and stay behind the counter."

10. "Each clerk is always assigned a section or department and except when necessarily selling goods in some other department—the clerk will always remain in that section BEHIND THE COUNTER. Please remember this as otherwise it will be necessary to remind you."

11. "Visiting among clerks is not encouraged and conversation with clerks should be confined to matters concerning the business of the store. Where two clerks are assigned to the same counter, they will remain at opposite ends and work towards the center."

12. "Each clerk is responsible for the section to which she is assigned. Each regular girl will furnish the manager with WANT LISTS and will keep counters, shelves and understock in good condition at all times. Girls will be required to know that their stock is in the stock room at all times."

13. "Saturday-girls will work under the direction of the regular girls and will be instantly removed upon the recommendation of the regular girls. Reports will be received from the regular girls weekly as to the fitness, efficiency, honesty, etc., of the Saturday-girls."

14. "An idle clerk is simply a reminder to the manager that he has too many clerks. There is always work to do in this store and we want the kind of clerks that can see the thing to do and do it."

15. "Sell no goods except for cash. Do not lay aside goods except those that are wrapped up and paid for. Put the name of the customer on the package and mark 'paid.'"

16. "Watch always for shoplifters and thieves and inform the manager promptly. Watch small boys and don't let them handle the toys."

17. "Always dust all counters, woodwork, etc., the first thing in the morning."

18. "Do not leave the counters or make preparations for leaving until the front doors are locked for closing."

19. "If your people call for you Saturday nights and other nights and wish to wait in the store for you—request them to do so without occupying your attention or the attention of some other clerk. You will instruct any young man who calls for you to escort you home, to meet you outside after the store has closed or after you are off duty."

20. "Be courteous and obliging in your treatment of all customers. The proper manner in which to address a customer is—'May I wait on you?' or 'Have you been waited on?' or 'Is someone waiting on you?' or 'What will you have today?'"

21. "Customers who are 'just looking' should be encouraged to look all the way through the store. Customers who make purchases up near the front of the store should be encouraged to visit all sections of the store. Always say 'Thank You.'"

22. "Conserve wrapping and notion bags. Always use the smallest size bags or paper that will allow you to wrap a neat, well-wrapped bundle. Use great care to see that all bundles are neatly wrapped. Always pick up any bags or wrapping paper you see on the floor. Use as little twine as possible."

23. "All salespeople are paid on a basis of what they sell. The scale will be shown you later."

24. "After making a sale, suggest other items to the customer."

25. "Make refunds and exchanges only upon the consent of the manager or his assistant. We do not exchange millinery, silk hosiery, yard goods of any kind or any other goods that are not returned in as good condition as taken out."

26. "No employees will be permitted to take merchandise from the counters, stock room, shelving, understocks, either for store or personal use. Every cent's worth of merchandise in the store is charged to the store's merchandise accounts. Small leaks cannot be tolerated. We will consider violations of this rule, a mark of dishonesty. If you want something for personal use, to take away with you, or for store use, see the manager."

27. "It is to the interest of our employees to observe the rules and report any failure on the part of other employees to observe them. All promotions are made from the people already employed. The manager will never keep long any employees who must be continually corrected."

28. "The manager will rank employees in the order in which they will assume authority in his absence. His appointments will be observed, and in the absence of superiors or seniors, the ranking clerk's authority must be respected."

"May I wait on you, please?" or "May I help, you?" could be the prelude to a business transaction in any of the five-and-ten-cent stores so popular in the early twentieth century. This greeting delivered by a salesgirl was followed by personal attention to the customer's shopping needs, whether her purchase amounted to five cents or five dollars.

Directors and Managers

Pennsylvania is often referred to as the birthplace of the dime store. Pennsylvania pioneers were S.S. Kresge, William T. Grant, John J. Newberry, G.C. Murphy, James Mack, Walter Show, S.H. Kress, and John G. McCrory. The only exception was F.W. Woolworth, who was born in New York but started in Pennsylvania.

S. S. Kresge had been inspired when he met F.W. Woolworth, but refused to go into partnership with Woolworth and joined instead into a partnership with J.G. McCrory.

A manager oversaw the progress of every store and was an active participant, leader, and representative of his store. He was also the implicit authority in his day-to-day responsibilities. Most of the store managers began at the bottom, starting in a stockroom and learning the fundamentals of the business. From there they advanced to assistant, working their way on up the ladder to superintendent, manager, buyer, or an executive position.

The importance of the store manager was historic. F.W. Woolworth and the founders of the Woolworth chain were store managers at the start.

The End of An Era

Many of the five-and-ten-cent stores had originally boomed in prewar downtowns and later became a familiar sight in suburban malls. By the late 1950s, suburban malls in most major cities drew customers away with free parking and easy access as newly developed shopping districts were built in most major cities. The five-and-ten had to compete for customers with other chain stores that carried much the same merchandise as was available in the five-and-ten.

As the dime stores became the victims of competition from the superstores, announcements began appearing daily in newspapers, drawing attention to closings, mergers, filings for Chapter 11 and/or liquidation of stock, and disposal of property. These icons were being replaced by megastores such as Target, Wal-Mart, and K-mart, where 52.5 million Americans now shop per month.

By 1987, there were only four known chain stores still in business. F.W. Woolworth, M.H. Lamston, McCrory, a division of the privately held Rapid-American Corporation, and Ben Franklin were still operating franchise stores.

In February 1997, McCrory liquidated 300 stores to generate immediate cash. The closing left approximately 161 stores operating under such names as McCrory, McLellan, H.L. Green, T.G. & Y., J.J. Newberry, and G.C. Murphy. Most of the remaining stores were in the eastern region of the United States and were evaluated to determine if they could generate enough profit to support a viable business plan.

On July 17, 1997, everyone heard the news: "Woolworth Closing All of its 5-and-10-Stores; 9,200 to be laid off." The following day, I purchased numerous newspapers, all with headlines announcing that the famous dime store era was officially coming to an end. Woolworth Corp. announced that it would close all 400 of its remaining five-and-dime stores nationwide and lay off 9,200 workers. Woolworth planned to convert 100 stores into Woolworth specialty stores. Fifty-five of the stores would become sporting-goods stores in Manhattan, New Jersey, and Florida. The only remaining stores will be 370 in Germany and 30 in Mexico. The company also plans to change its corporate name from Woolworth Corp. sometime in the near future.

The Glassware

The majority of glassware illustrated here was manufactured by the Anchor Hocking Company of Lancaster, Ohio. It is often referred to as "Depression Glass," a phrase created during the 1960s that symbolizes inexpensive glass made before, during, and after the Depression.

Artistic Cut Glass was from The Standard Glass Manufacturing Co., Lancaster, Ohio, with facilities in Canal Winchester and Breman, Ohio. Another symbol of glassware referred to during the 1940s was "Artistic Cut, The World's Greatest Cut Glass Values."

The Standard Glass Manufacturing Co. recommended that dime stores provide variety in their glassware department. They suggested offering at least two lines of cut ware, one in a machine cutting and the other in a better design that was cut by hand. Dime stores were reminded to establish reputations for their stores as the place where a variety of glassware and gifts was available.

Matched crystal stemware was shipped from facilities in West Virginia. No company trademark was provided. This stemware was a fine quality, clear, thin-blown crystal. Bearing smooth edges, the pieces were tall with graceful shapes, beautifully cut and smartly styled. They were promoted to the retailer as extraordinary values to sell at low popular prices.

Moonstone Tableware

Issued January 12, 1943, "Moonstone" was a line of expensive looking glassware in Early American Hobnail pattern, the latest addition of the Anchor Hocking Glass Company, Lancaster, Ohio. Often referred to as "Opalescent Hobnail," this popular glassware was ideal for gifts and tableware and sold at sensationally low prices. Its advertising noted that "Dime store counters were not complete unless they included 'Moonstone.'"

"Issued" does not necessarily mean the date of introduction or manufacturer of the item, but rather the date the paperwork was issued to the stores.

Left: "Moonstone" cup and 6-1/4" saucer. Retailed 10¢ set. Right: "Moonstone" 6 oz. sherbet and 6-1/4" sherbet plate. Retailed for 10¢ set. Cup/Saucer $15-$20. Sherbet/Saucer $15-$20.

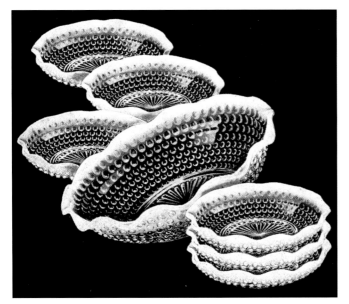

The seven piece "Moonstone" dessert set consisted of: one 9-1/2" bowl and six 5-1/2" dessert bowls. Retailed 50¢-59¢ set. $50-$60 set.

Left: "Moonstone" 5-1/2" dessert. Retailed 5¢. Right: "Moonstone" 10 oz. goblet Retailed 10¢. Dessert $15-$20. Goblet $15-$20.

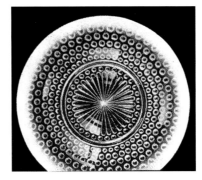

"Moonstone" 8-3/8" luncheon plate. Retailed 10¢. $15-$20.

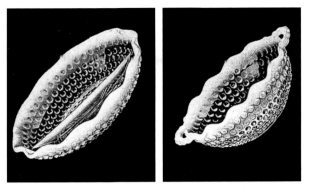

Left: "Moonstone" 7-3/4" divided relish. Retailed 10¢-15¢. Right: "Moonstone" crimped handled 6-1/2" bowl. Retailed 72¢. Relish $10-$15. Bowl $15-$20.

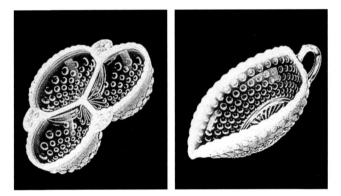

Left: "Moonstone" clover leaf 6-3/4" dish. Retailed 80¢. Right: "Moonstone" heart shaped 6-1/2" bonbon dish. Retailed 75¢. Clover $15-$20. Heart $15-$20.

Left: "Moonstone" 7-3/4" flat bowl. Retailed 75¢. Right: "Moonstone" open sugar and creamer. Retailed 72¢ each. Bowl $15-$20. Sugar/Creamer $15-$20 set.

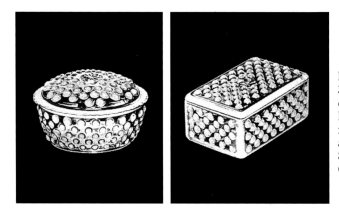

Left: "Moonstone" 4-3/4" puff box and cover. Retailed 80¢. Right: "Moonstone" 5" x 3-3/8" cigarette jar and cover. Retailed 80¢. Puff $25-$30. Cigarette $25-$30.

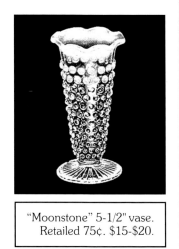

"Moonstone" 5-1/2" vase. Retailed 75¢. $15-$20.

"Moonstone" 6" covered candy jar. Retailed 20¢. $25-$30.

This cologne bottle has the original paper label on the bottom, reading
"Moonstone Hobnail Cologne by Wrisley New York - Chicago 9 oz., Bottle
Hand Made By American Craftsmen." Also shown is a "Moonstone"
covered candy jar. *Davis Collection*. Cologne $15-$20. Jar $25-$30.

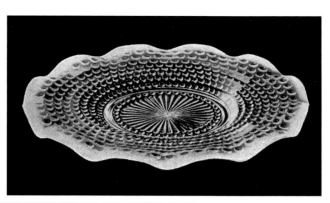

"Moonstone" 10-3/4" sandwich plate. Retailed 20¢. $20-$25.

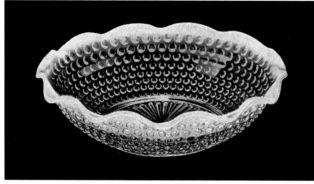

"Moonstone" 9-1/2" crimped bowl. Retailed 20¢. $15-$20.

Four piece "Moonstone" buffet set. Includes: one 9-1/2" bowl, one 10-3/4" plate and two 4-1/4" candleholders. Retailed 50¢ set. $50-$60 set.

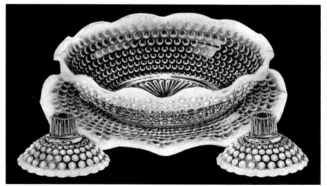

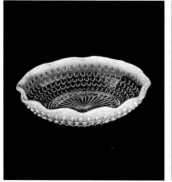

Left: "Moonstone" crimped 5-1/2" dessert. Retailed 5¢. Right: "Moonstone" 4-1/4" candleholder. Retailed 5¢. Dessert $5-$10. Candleholder $15-$20 pair.

Anchor Hocking "Milk White Anchorglass®," approximately 9-3/4" with gold trim. Divided relish or fruit tray with original paper label. Lancaster, Ohio U.S.A. Davis Collection. $15-$20.

An original carton for a sugar and creamer from "Anchor Hocking Glass Corp. Lancaster, Ohio." *Davis Collection.* $20-$25 complete.

Anchor Hocking "22K Gold Trimmed Anchorglass®" sugar and creamer with original carton. *Davis Collection.* $20-$25 complete.

This original Anchorglass® advertisement appeared in the May, 1954 issue of *Family Circle*. Advertised as brand new 4-piece sets in "Tulip," "Black Polka Dots," or "Red Polka Dots," these sets were available at your favorite chain store. *Advertisement Courtesy of Davis Collection.* Bowls $40-$50 per complete set.

Anchorglass *takes the splatter out of mixing!*

At last! AMAZING DEEP-BOWL SET
DESIGNED FOR *Splash-proof* MIXING!

TULIP SET...1, 2, 3, 4 QT. BOWLS SMARTLY PACKED IN GIFT CARTON

4-PIECE SETS ABOUT $2.95

DEEP sides and tapered shape of these bowls prevent splashing! No more wiping splatters from walls, counter, floor!

You'll find these brand-new Anchor-glass splash-proof bowls rest on a good, firm base; perfectly balanced for tip-proof beating. Whether you use a wooden spoon, wire whisk, hand beater or portable electric mixer, you can reach every bit of batter without fear of splashing.

Notice the tapered sides. They make these bowls easy to hold, pour from, clean. You can even bake in amazing Anchorglass! So handsome, you'll use them as serving bowls, too!

See these remarkable mixing bowls wherever glass is sold. If your dealer does not have them in stock, he can get them for you by writing Anchor Hocking Glass Corporation.

• BLACK POLKA DOTS
1, 2, 3, 4 QT. BOWLS

• RED POLKA DOTS
1, 2, 3, 4 QT. BOWLS

Smartly packed in gift carton, about $2.95

Look for the name **Anchorglass** Guaranteed by Good Housekeeping

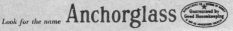

A PRODUCT OF ANCHOR HOCKING GLASS CORPORATION, LANCASTER, OHIO

Another Anchorglass® advertisment, this one from the April, 1954 issue of *Family Circle*. The ad announced a new dinnerware service for four, available in "Gray Laurel," "Peach Lustre," and "Jade-Ite." *Advertisement Courtesy of Davis Collection.* $50-$60 per complete set.

Anchorglass *makes your dream-table come true!*

Imagine! A Dinnerware Service for 4...RICH, GRAY LAUREL...

GOLDEN PEACH LUSTRE...GLOWING JADE-ITE

about $279 *complete*

...and they are heat-proof
...will not "craze"!

Now! You can set your table—company style—with your choice of the glamorous new dinnerware patterns pictured here! And, wonder of wonders, these gleaming pieces are as strong and practical as they are low in price.

Don't put off the luxury of setting a lovely table one second longer. See this lovely Anchorglass dinnerware, wherever glassware is sold. If your dealer does not have this tableware in stock, he can get it for you by writing Anchor Hocking Glass Corporation.

All dinnerware pieces are available individually in open stock at low prices...for instance, cups and saucers, only 10¢ each!

Guaranteed by Good Housekeeping

Look for the name **Anchorglass**

A PRODUCT OF ANCHOR HOCKING GLASS CORPORATION • LANCASTER, OHIO

Fancy Glassware

This useful modern shape glassware in an attractive "Prescut" design was manufactured by Anchor Hocking.

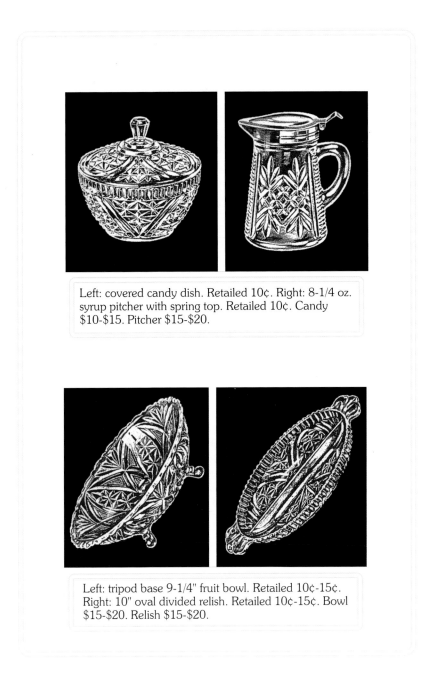

Left: covered candy dish. Retailed 10¢. Right: 8-1/4 oz. syrup pitcher with spring top. Retailed 10¢. Candy $10-$15. Pitcher $15-$20.

Left: tripod base 9-1/4" fruit bowl. Retailed 10¢-15¢. Right: 10" oval divided relish. Retailed 10¢-15¢. Bowl $15-$20. Relish $15-$20.

Left: 8" deep bowl. Retailed 10¢-15¢. Right: 7-1/2" three part dish. Retailed 10¢. Bowl $15-$20. Dish $15-$20.

Left: 10-3/4" fan tray. Retailed 10¢-15¢. Right: 12 oz. milk pitcher. Retailed 10¢. Tray $15-$20. Pitcher $15-$20.

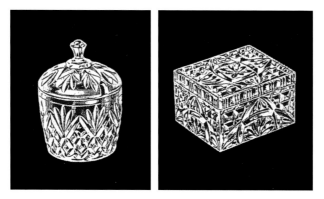

Left: covered marmalade. Retailed 10¢. Right: covered jewel box. Retailed 10¢-15¢. Marmalade $15-$20. Box $20-$25.

Left: covered round puff 4-5/8" box. Retailed 10¢. Right: 4-3/4" perfume bottle and stopper. Retailed 10¢. Box $20-$25. Perfume $25-$30.

Left: 12" cake plate. Retailed 15¢-20¢. Right: 12" partitioned relish. Retailed 15¢-20¢. $15-$20 each.

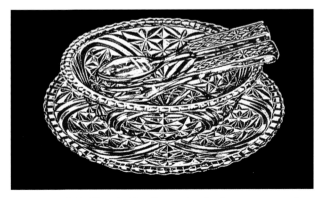

10-1/2" Salad bowl, 12-1/2" sandwich plate, spoon and fork. Sold as a set or individually. $50-$60 set.

Candy jar, 6-3/4" with cover. Retailed 25¢. $15-$20 complete.

Left: shallow 7-1/2" bowl. Retailed 5¢ or 2/15¢. Right: 8" salad plate. Retailed 5¢. Bowl $10-$15. Plate $10-$15.

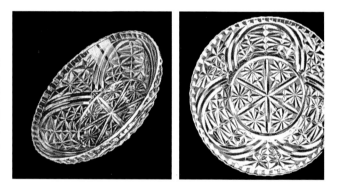

Seven piece "Hostess Set" consisting of 14" crystal tray, five triangular ruby dishes, one crystal mayonnaise. $75-$100 complete.

Left: handled 6" jelly.
Retailed 5¢. Right: tab
handle 6" nut dish.
Retailed 5¢. Jelly $10-
$15. Nut $10-$15.

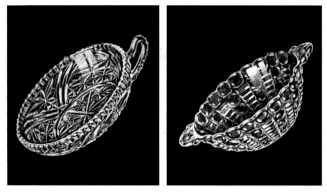

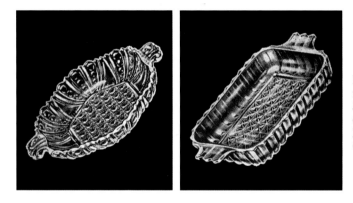

Left: hexagonal 6"
mint tray. Retailed
5¢. Right: oblong
6" tray. Retailed 5¢.
Mint $10-$15.
Oblong $10-$15.

Left: Oval 7-3/4" olive
dish. Retailed 5¢.
Right: open sugar and
creamer. Retailed 5¢.
Dish $10-$15. Sugar/
Creamer $15-$20 set.

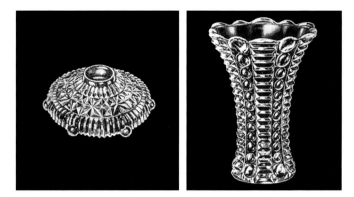

Left: 4" candleholder. Retailed 5¢. Right: 4-3/4" vase. Retailed 5¢. Candleholder $5-$10 each. Vase $10-$15.

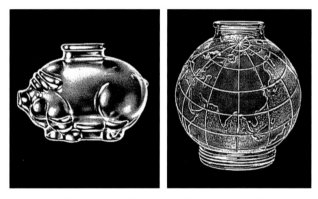

Left: 4-3/8" pig bank. Right: 4-1/8" world bank. Retailed 5¢ each. Pig $15-$20. World $15-$20.

Left: plain 3-3/4" Liberty Bell bank. Retailed 5¢. Right: 3-3/4" Liberty Bell bank, decorated in red, white, and blue. Retailed 10¢. Plain $15-$20. Decorated $25-$30.

Left: 7" hurricane lamp. Retailed 10¢-15¢. Right: 5-1/4" mold etched design bowl. Retailed 3/10¢. Lamp $10-$15. Bowl $15-$20.

Left: 9-1/2 oz. tall pressed tumbler. Retailed 3/15¢. Right: 3-7/8" footed sherbet. Retailed 3/10¢. Tumbler $15-$20. Sherbet $10-$15.

Fruit and Dessert Sets

These sets were also sold individually or as complete sets. Issued January 12, 1943.

Two piece blossom dessert set, consists of: one 4-3/4" blossom bowl and one 8-1/4" leaf plate. Retailed 10¢ set. $25-$30 complete set.

Seven piece crystal glass "Fruit or Dessert" set. Consists of: one 7-3/4" bowl and six 4-1/2" desserts. $40-$50 complete.

Seven piece crystal glass "Fruit or Dessert" set. Consists of: one 8-1/2" bowl and six 4-1/2" desserts. $40-$50 complete.

Seven piece crystal glass "Berry Set." Consists of: one 8-1/4" bowl and six 4-1/2" desserts. $50-$60 complete.

Seven piece crystal glass "Leaf Dessert" set. Consists of: one
8-1/2" bowl and six 4-1/2" desserts. Retailed 45¢-49¢ set.
$40-$50 complete.

Seven piece crystal glass "Berry Set." Consists of: one
8-1/2" bowl and six 4-1/2" desserts. Retailed 29¢-35¢.
$40-$50 complete.

Seven piece ruby glass "Berry Set." Retailed 40¢-50¢. Consists of: one 8-1/2" bowl and six 4-1/2" desserts. $100-$125 complete.

Four piece "Salad Set." Consists of: one 10-5/8" ruby console bowl, one 12-1/2" sandwich plate, spoon and fork. $75-$100 complete.

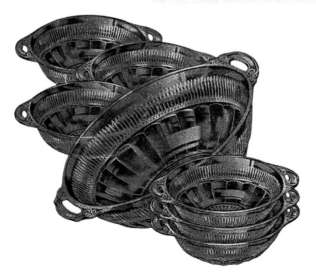

Seven piece ruby open tab handled glass "Berry Set." Retailed 35¢-39¢. Consists of: one 8" bowl and six 4-1/2" desserts. $125-$150 complete.

Ruby Glassware

This rich looking glassware was available only from Anchor Hocking and was sold at affordable prices in the local five-and-ten-cent stores.

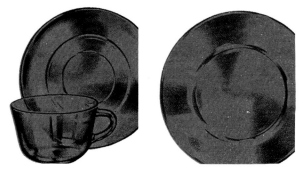

4" x 2-1/2" cup and 6" saucer. Retailed 5¢. Right: 8" salad plate. Retailed 5¢. Also available was a 9-1/4" dinner plate, not shown. Cup/Saucer $15-$20 complete. Plate $10-$15.

7-1/2" soup plate. Retailed 10¢. Right: 6 oz. footed sherbet. Retailed 5¢. Plate $10-$15. Sherbet $15-$20.

Left: 9 oz. stem goblet. Retailed 10¢. Right: open sugar and creamer. Retailed 10¢ each. Goblet $25-$30. Sugar/Creamer $35-$40 complete.

In 1943, these tumblers were known as "NEW RUBY TUMBLERS." They were advertised as having the most spectacular decorated silverine white on ruby glass ever offered. The eye-catching decorations enhanced the richness of the ruby color in the glass. These were thin blown glasses with

reinforced edges that resisted chipping. Top, from left: 9-1/2 oz. "Laurel Wreath" tumbler; 9-1/2 oz. "Ship Design" tumbler. Bottom, from left: 9-1/2 oz. "Wild Geese" tumbler; 9-1/2 oz. "Wild Flower" tumbler. Retailed 5¢ each. Laurel $10-$15. Ship $10-$15. Geese $10-$15. Flower $10-$15.

Left: gold band and hairline decoration on 9-1/2 oz. tumbler. Right: plain ruby 9-1/2 oz. tumbler. Retailed 5¢ each. Gold $10-$15. Plain $5-$10.

Left: 9-1/2 oz. hobnail pattern ruby tumbler. Retailed 5¢.
Right: 60 oz. hobnail pattern ruby pitcher. Retailed 15¢.
Tumbler $15-$20. Pitcher $35-$40.

Left: heavy pressed 9 oz. table tumbler. This was also
offered in a 5 oz. fruit juice. Retailed 3/10¢. Right: 60 oz.
heavy pressed pitcher. Retailed 3/10¢. Table Tumbler $10-
$15. Fruit Juice $5-$10. Pitcher $20-$25.

Left: 9 oz. tumbler. Retailed 5¢. Right: 15 hour candle
tumbler. Retailed 5¢. Tumbler $10-$15. Candle $5-$10.

Ivory Tableware

The Anchor Hocking "Ivory Tableware" was an ivory glass that had the color of semi-porcelain and the translucence of fine china. It was tempered by a special process that produced a combination of beauty, strength, and durability. Issued January 12, 1943.

Left: 3-5/8" x 2-5/16" cup and 5-5/8" saucer. Right: 9-1/4" dinner plate. Cup/Saucer $15-$20 complete. Plate $20-$25.

Left: 5-1/2" cereal bowls. Right: 8-3/4" vegetable bowl. Cereal $5-$10. Vegetable $25-$30.

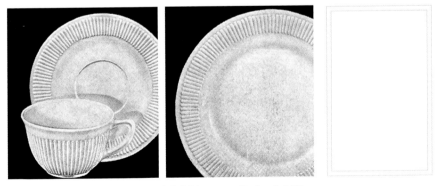

Left: 3-3/4" x 2-5/16" cup and 5-5/8" saucer. Right: 9-1/4" dinner plate. These are a different pattern than the bowls shown in the previous photo. Pattern names were not provided. Cup/Saucer $15-$20 complete. Plate $20-$25.

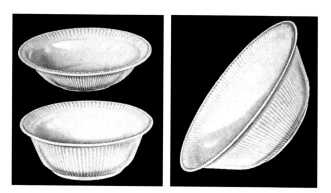

Left: 5-1/2" cereal bowls. Right: 8-3/4" vegetable bowl. Still a different pattern than those previous. Cereal $5-$10. Vegetable $25-$30.

St. Denis cup and 5-7/8" saucer. $10-$20.

Vases

These 9" vases were decorated in either Chinese red, blue, or plain ivory. Vases $15-$20 each.

Additional 9" vases were available and decorated in either red or blue flamingo decoration. Vases $15-$20 each.

Left: plain ruby glass 9" vases. Right: decorated ruby 9" vase. $15-$20 each.

Left: crystal glass 7" vase. Right: 8-3/4" crystal glass vase. $10-$15 each.

Ivy bowls were available in 4" and 6" crystal and/or ruby. $5-$10 each.

Ivory Glass
(Plain and Decorated)

The following items were often displayed in the horticulture department.

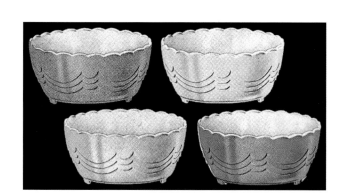

These 5-1/4" footed bulb bowls were available in plain ivory, tangerine, yellow, green, and blue. $15-$20 each.

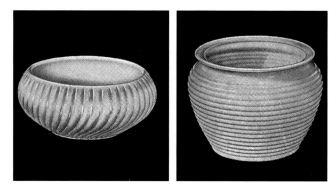

6-1/4" plain ivory bulb bowl. Right: 6-3/4" plain ivory bulb bowl. $5-$10 each.

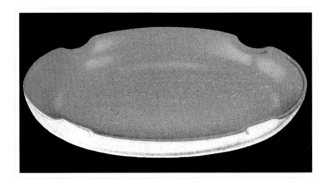

The 10-5/8" flower tray was available in plain ivory, peach, yellow, green, and blue. $20-$25 each.

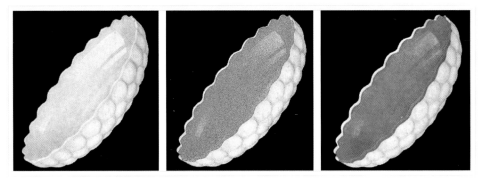

These smaller (8-1/2") flower trays were also available in plain ivory, peach, yellow, green, and blue. $15-$20 each.

This "Flower Block" in crystal was available in either 3-1/8" or 4-1/2". $5-$10 each.

Waterford Tableware

Waterford tableware was a brilliant diamond crystal pattern, having both style and quality. It was manufactured by Anchor Hocking.

Left: Cup and 6" saucer. Right: 6 oz. sherbet and 6" sherbet plate. Cup/Saucer $20-$25 complete. Sherbet/ Plate $20-$25 complete.

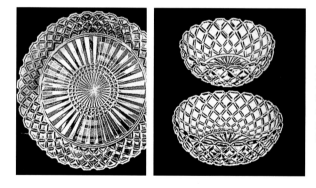

Left: 7-1/8" salad plate. Right: 4-1/3" desserts. Also available was a 9-1/2" dinner plate and 5-1/2" nappy not shown. Salad $5-$10. Dessert $5-$10.

Left: 8-1/4" bowl. Right: 10-1/8" cake plate. Bowl $15-$20. Plate $25-$30.

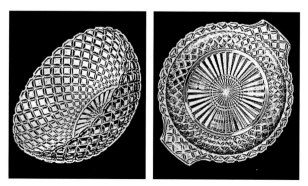

Waterford tableware: covered sugar with creamer, 4" ruby tops salt and pepper shakers, 6-1/2" butter and cover. Cream/Sugar $25-$30. Shakers $15-$20 set. Butter $30-$35.

Left: 10 oz. goblet. Right: 10 oz. footed tumbler. Waterford tableware was the world's largest selling glass tableware line. Goblet $10-$15. Tumbler $10-$15.

Ice lipped 90 oz. pitcher. Also available was a 12 oz. fruit juice jug. Pitcher $50-$60. Jug $40-$50.

Left: 4" coaster.
Right: 4" ash tray.
Coaster $10-$15.
Tray $30-$40.

Sandwich plate, 14". Also shown is a seven piece "Hostess Set" consisting of a 14" crystal tray, five triangular dishes, one crystal mayonnaise. $50-$100 complete.

Fire-King Oven Glass

Fire-King was guaranteed against heat breakage for two years. This beautifully designed tableware could be used in the oven, on the table, and in the refrigerator. Fire-King could be purchased as a 16-piece tableware set, a 16-piece luncheon set, or a 25-piece dinner set.

Left: cup and saucer. Right: 7" salad plate. Cup/Saucer $20-$25 complete. Plate $15-$20.

Left: 9-1/4" dinner plate. Right 8" soup plate. Also available was a 9-1/4" grill plate (photograph not available). Dinner $20-$25. Soup $15-$20. Grill $30-$35.

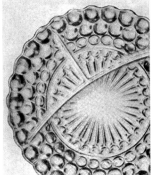

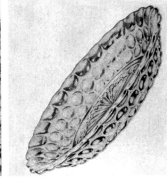

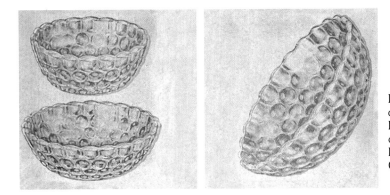

Left: 4-1/8" small dessert or soup. Right: 5-1/2" cereal or soup. Dessert $10-$15. Cereal $15-$20.

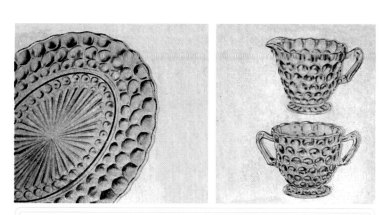

Left: 4-1/2" fruit plate. Right: open sugar and creamer. Plate $10-$15. Sugar/Creamer $30-$40 complete.

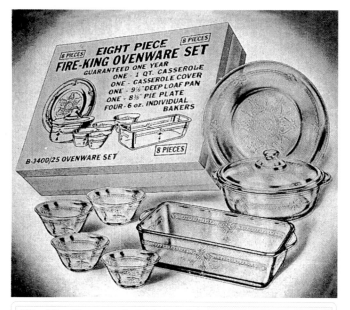

"Fire-King Ovenware" eight piece introductory set, consisted of one 1-quart casserole with knob cover, one 9-1/8" deep loaf pan, one 8-3/8" pie plate, four 6 oz. individual bakers. Packaged in individual carton and issued January 12, 1943. Due to the shortage of metal, the demand for glass cooking utensils was increasing daily. "Fire-King Ovenware" was profitable and low in price, offering a quick turnover and guaranteed sales. $100-$125 complete.

"Fire-King Ovenware" ten piece introductory set, consisted of one 1-1/2 quart casserole with knob cover, two 8-3/8" pie plate, and six 6 oz. individual bakers. Packaged in individual carton. $125-$150 complete.

"Fire-King Oven Glass" three piece utility bowl set, consisted of one 6-7/8" utility bowl, one 8-3/8" utility bowl, and one 10-1/8" utility bowl. $90-$100 complete.

"Fire-King Oven Glass" 9-5/8 pie plate. $25-$30.

"Fire-King Oven Glass" 1 quart round casserole with knob lid. $45-$50.

"Fire-King Oven Glass" 2 quart round casserole with pie plate cover. $50-$65.

"Fire-King Oven Glass" 2 quart open baker. $30-$40.

"Fire-King Oven Glass" individual 10 oz. casserole and cover. $35-$45.

"Fire-King Oven Glass" 5-3/8" x 1-7/8" individual pie dish. $20-$25.

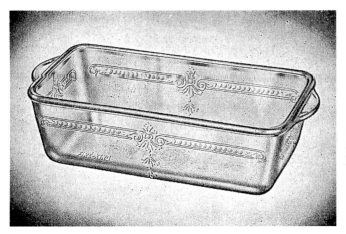

"Fire-King Oven Glass" 9-1/8" deep loaf pan. $20-$25.

"Fire-King Oven Glass" 10-1/2" utility tray. $20-$25.

"Fire-King Oven Glass" 1 pint square open baker and a 4-1/2" x 5" jar and cover. Square $15-$20. Jar/Cover $20-$25.

"Fire-King Oven Glass" 5-1/2" x 9-1/4" jar and cover, shown with deep loaf pan (also shown on page 57, top). Jar/Cover $25-$30. Loaf $20-$25.

"Fire-King Oven Glass" 16 oz. measuring cup. $40-$50.

Left: 8 oz. measuring cup. Right: percolator top. Cup $10-$15. Top $5-$10.

"Fire-King Oven Glass" 6 oz. deep custard cups. $5-$10 each.

"Fire-King Oven Glass" 5 oz. shallow custard cups. $4-$8 each.

"Fire-King Oven Glass" 6 oz. individual baker-servers. $4-$8 each.

Left: "Fire-King Oven Glass" 8 oz. and 4 oz. nursing bottles. Right: 7 oz. heavy coffee mug. Bottle 8 oz. $15-$20. Bottle 4 oz. $10-$15. Mug $20-$25.

Crystal clear "Fire-King ® Ovenware" was advertised as "The Most Famous Name in Glass" in 1952.

Gives you more...for less!

You can't buy finer glass ovenware at any price. You *can* pay more—20% to 40% more. But why pay more when only FIRE-KING gives you all these features:

★ Guaranteed 2 years against oven breakage.
★ Choice of 22 items—in sets or open stock.
★ Crystal-clear color for visibility.
★ Smoother surfaces rinse clean, easily, quickly.
★ Good Housekeeping Seal of Approval.

Only FIRE-KING offers you so much for so little cost!

Another Fine Product by
ANCHOR HOCKING
The Most Famous Name in Glass!

**SAVE EVEN MORE
BY THE SET!**

• 1½ Qt. Casserole   • 5" x 9" Deep Loaf Pan
  Knob Cover   • Six 6 oz. Desserts
• 6½" x 10½" Utility   • 9" Pie Plate
  Baking Pan   • 1 Qt. Pudding Pan

Complete 12-piece set about $2.39.

ANCHOR HOCKING GLASS CORPORATION
LANCASTER, OHIO

Guaranteed by Good Housekeeping

This ad describing original "Fire-King ® Ovenware" as "Another Fine Product by Anchor Hocking" appeared in a leading magazine in 1953.

Fish Globes, Oil Lamps, and
Kitchen Founts

Anchor Hocking noted that many merchants failed to realize the demand for fish globes. Customers were inclined to look for them only where goldfish were sold because other stores did not stock them. Fish globes sold all year round. They were profit numbers and a spread of sizes were displayed at all time.

Left to right: 2 gallon drum shape fish globe, 1 gallon drum shape fish globe, 1/2 gallon drum shape fish globe, and 1 quart drum shape fish globe. $15-$30 each.

Left to right: 2 gallon squat shape fish globe, 1 gallon squat shape fish globe, 1/2 gallon squat shape fish globe, and 1 quart squat shape fish globe. $10-$40 each.

Standard lamp, sewing lamps, and kitchen fount. Lamps and kitchen founts were in greater demand in 1943 than ever before. Stores were reminded to prepare for an increase in sales and get these on their counters, as they were good money makers. $20-$25 each.

Tumblers and Glasses

These pressed water tumblers in crystal glass were manufactured by Anchor Hocking. They were of medium weight and calculated to hold up best under hard usage.

Table tumblers, 9 oz. $5-$10 each.

Left: 9 oz. table tumbler. Right: 9 oz. square bottom table tumbler. $5-$10 each.

Left: 9 oz. table tumbler. Right: 8-1/2 oz. optic tumbler. $5-$10 each.

These beautiful "Prescut" patterns were available in 10 oz. tumblers. $5-$10 each.

Left: 10 oz. footed Waterford tumbler. Right: 9 oz. Georgian tumbler. $5-$10 each.

Pressed fruit juice glasses, 5 oz. each. $5-$10 each.

Pressed fruit juice glasses, 5 oz. each. Right glass has a square bottom base. $5-$10 each.

Pressed ice tea glasses, 12 oz.. each. $10-$15 each.

"Prescut" 13 oz. ice tea glass. $5-$10.

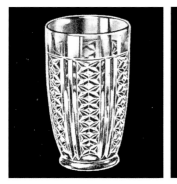
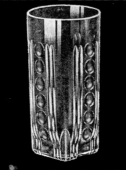

Pressed ice tea glasses, 13 oz.. each. Right glass has a square bottom base. $5-$10 each.

Hotel, Restaurant, Bar
and Fountain Glassware

Here are tumblers that needed no introduction. They were used universally by restaurants, hotels, lunch stands, and soda fountains. Tumblers were crystal glass, highly polished, medium weight, and heavy pressed.

Hotel tumbler, 9 oz. barrel bottom. $5-$10.

Left: optic cupped 8-1/2 oz. tumbler. Right: plain straight 8 oz. tumbler. $5-$10 each.

Left: fluted cupped 8 oz. tumbler. Right: optic 9 oz. tumbler. $5-$10 each.

Left: ice tea 1 oz. glass. Right: 5 oz. tulip sundae glass. Tea $5-$10. Tulip $15-$20.

Left: 10 oz. beer mug. Right: 8 oz. beer mug. $10-$15 each.

Crystal whiskey glasses. $5-$10 each.

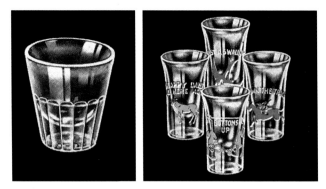

Left: 1 oz. whiskey glass. Right: 1 oz. decorated whiskey glasses. Plain $5-$10. Decorated $20-$25 each.

Left: 1 oz. straight wine glass. Right: 2 oz. footed wine glass. Straight $5-$10. Footed $10-$15.

Left: 3-1/2 oz. fruit juice glass. Right: 7-1/2 oz. old-fashioned cocktail glass. Juice $10-$15. Cocktail $5-$10.

Left: 3-1/2 oz. colonial sherbet. Right: 7 oz. sherbet and 6" sherbet plate. Also available was an 8" salad plate (photograph not available.) Colonial $5-$10. Sherbet/Plate $20-$25 complete.

Left: 5 oz. straight shell tumbler. Right: 7 oz. straight shell tumbler. $5-$10 each.

Left: 9 oz. straight shell tumbler. Right: 12 oz. straight shell tumbler. $5-$10 each.

Left: 5 oz. fancy fruit juice. Right: 9 oz. fancy table tumbler. $5-$10 each.

Left: 5 oz. fancy fruit juice. Right: 12 oz. fancy ice tea, $5-$10 each.

Left: 5 oz. bulged shell glass. Right: 8 oz. tall bulged glass. $5-$10 each.

Left: 8 oz. regular bulged tumbler. Right: 10 oz. tall bulged tumbler. $5-$10 each.

Left: 6-1/2 oz. cola tumbler. Right: 10 oz. and 12 oz. bell soda tumblers. $10-$15 each.

The most popular shaped glass, 12 oz. ice tea. This shape was available in whiskey, wine, fruit juice, table tumbler, and ice tea. $5-$10 each.

Left: Crackled Crystal Design 14 oz. ice tea glass. Right: 80 oz. Crackled Crystal Design ice lip pitcher. Glass $15-$18. Pitcher $20-$25.

Left: 60 oz. blown, crystal glass water pitcher. Right: 80 oz. blown, crystal glass ice lip pitcher. $20-$25 each.

Left: 60 oz. blown, crystal glass pitcher. Right: 80 oz. blown, crystal glass ice lip pitcher. $20-$25 each.

Left: 60 oz. blown, crystal glass pitcher. Right: 12 oz. blown, crystal glass pitcher. $20-$25 each.

Left: 37 oz. embossed floral pattern milk pitcher. Right: 60 oz. crystal tankard jug. $20-$25 each.

This 60 oz. ice lip pitcher was the most popular pitcher sold. It featured heavy crystal glass, spiral flute design, ice lip, smooth handle, and perfect balance. $20-$25.

Refrigerator and Kitchen Glassware

Through the proper display of these items, dime stores were to remind customers of their need for this crystal refrigerator glassware. A large window display and the proper counter set-up would increase sales.

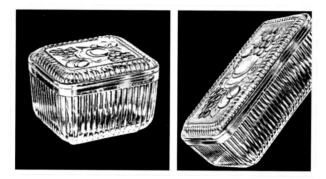

Left: 4-3/5" x 5" refrigerator jar and cover. Right: 5" x 8-3/4" refrigerator jar and cover. Left $5-$10. Right $10-$15.

This six piece refrigerator set consists of one 4-7/8" jar and cover, one 5-1/4" jar and cover, and one 6" jar and cover. $30-$40 complete.

Left: 1 quart refrigerator bottle and cap. Right: 2 quart refrigerator bottle and cap. $10-$15 each.

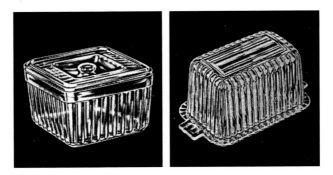

Left: 5" square refrigerator jar and cover. Right: 1 lb. butter and cover. Jar $5-$10. Butter $15-$20.

This chiller and cover
held 54 oz. $15-$20.

This four piece kitchen bowl set consists of one 4-7/8" bowl,
one 5-1/4" bowl, and one 6" bowl, and one 7-1/2" bowl. $35-
$45 complete.

Left: 1/2 gallon storage jar with green lid. Right: 1/2 pint provision jar with glass cover. Half Gallon $15-$20. Pint $20-$25.

These 1 pint decorated provision jars with glass covers were available with various flower motifs. $30-$40 each.

Left: 7" crystal orange juice extractor. Right: 6" crystal lemon juice extractor. Orange $10-$15. Lemon $20-$25.

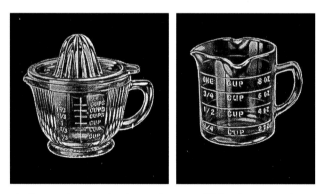

Left: crystal measuring jug and reamer. Right: 8 oz. crystal measuring cup. Jug/Reamer $40-$50 complete. Cup $5-$10.

Left: 2-1/8" percolator top. Right: 3-1/8" salt and pepper shakers with red plastic tops. Top $1-$5. Shakers $5-$10 complete.

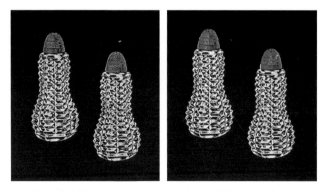

Left: 4-1/8" salt and pepper shakers with green plastic tops. Right: 4-1/8" salt and pepper shakers with red plastic tops. $10-$15 complete.

Left: 3-1/4" salt and pepper shakers with red metal tops.
Right: 5-1/4" crystal handled bowl. Shakers $5-$10.
Bowl $10-$15.

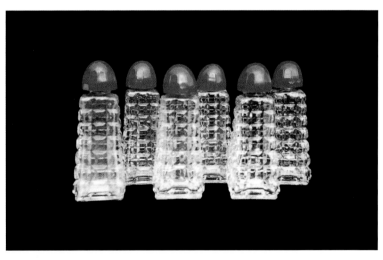

This selection of G.C. Murphy Shakers salt and pepper shakers with
red plastic lids have the original "Murphy's 10¢" price sticker on the
bottom of each shaker. *Schneider Collection*. $5-$6 each set.

Left: 6 oz. oil bottle with stopper. Right: 8-1/4 oz. syrup pitcher with spring top. Bottle $5-$10. Syrup $15-$20.

This ivory nested kitchen bowl set consists of one 5-1/4" bowl, one 6" bowl, one 7-1/2" bowl, and one 9" bowl. Bowls could be purchased individually. $50-$60 complete set.

This ivory nested kitchen bowl set with red decoration consists of one 5-1/4" bowl, one 6" bowl, one 7-1/2" bowl, and one 9" bowl. Bowls could be purchased individually. $75-$80 complete set.

★ SERVE ★ AT HOME

SAVE FOOD WITH

Kontānerettes

SOLD AT LEADING DEPARTMENT STORES

REFRIGERATOR AND PANTRY JARS ON REVOLVING TRAY

YOU CAN SERVE your country and save with handy, crystal clear, revolving Kontānerettes. Preserve the freshness of left-overs, vegetables, fruits and juices. The savings you'll make will get you many needed extras. Save refrigerator space and time, too. Contents quickly seen. Easy selection of jars with revolving, ball-bearing tray. Four sizes: 3-jar set 85c; 4-jar $1; 5-jar $2.50; 6-jar $3.50 (slightly higher Denver and west).

SOME PREFER CONSERV-O-JARS

Like Kontānerettes, on revolving ball-bearing tray, but with flat covers, handles at side. One style only, Model 502 (5-jar set) $2.50 (slightly higher Denver and west).

Free RECIPE BOOK

Get thrifty recipes for left-overs in 16-page booklet "Economizing on Economy." Send for it today.

INDIANA GLASS CO., DUNKIRK, IND.

PRESSED • BLOWN • CRYSTAL • DECORATED GLASSWARE

INDIANA *Glassware*

This original advertisement for the revolving "Kontanerettes" appeared in a May, 1942 magazine. Indiana Glass Co., Dunkirk, Indiana. $50-$60 complete.

NOW LET EVERY PYREX DISH BRAND **SERVE YOU ALL THESE WAYS!**

1. **TASTY MEATS AND FISH!** Your Pyrex utility dish cooks roasts, fish, chops, all kinds of main courses. Cook, serve, store leftovers in same dish with no extra dishwashing! 10½" size, only **50¢**

IN times like these you can keep every modern Pyrex dish busy! For example, just check all the ways you can use this one! Each smart Pyrex dish can be used for a dozen appetizing recipes. And you can serve and store each food in the same sparkling clear utensil it was cooked in. Pyrex ware cooks better, and faster —saving fuel. It washes easier! Choose Pyrex ware to help you serve better meals for less money!

2. **TEMPTING VEGETABLE DISHES!** See how this Pyrex dish dresses up vegetables and makes them more appetizing. Tomatoes stuffed with corn and peas; candied sweet potatoes; individual Hubbard squashes; a dozen others!

3. **CRISP SALADS!** Ever think of using your utility dish as a salad bowl, or for serving chopped-up fruits? Adds sparkle and charm to any table, and washes clean as a whistle with no effort at all!

4. **DELICIOUS DESSERTS!** Ginger bread, cakes, puddings, custards are just a few of the many good things you can prepare and serve in this glistening Pyrex ware utility dish!

EVERY GLEAMING DISH HAS A DOZEN USES!

Amazing Pyrex Utensils that fear no fire!

NEW deep "Flavor Saver" pie plate with handles. Fluted edge keeps juice and flavor in your pies! Many extra uses. 10" size..only **45¢**

NEW Pyrex bowls perfect for mixing, baking, serving and storing! Nest together to save space. Set of three—1, 1½ and 2½ qt. sizes..only **95¢**

RIGHT OVER THE FLAME Liquid levels always visible. Modern Pyrex Flameware saucepan, 1 qt. **$1 65**

PYREX
BRAND
OVENWARE FLAMEWARE

"PYREX" IS A REGISTERED TRADE-MARK ... LOOK FOR IT FOR YOUR OWN PROTECTION

This original Pyrex® advertisement appeared in a 1940s publication. These modern cooking utensils were available at your favorite store and—as the ad noted—every gleaming dish had "a dozen uses!" $3-$5 each.

Who says a bride can't cook?

...she can *easily* if you give her modern Pyrex Ware

FASTER-BAKING PYREX pie plate turns out "picture" pies and flaky crusts every time. No clinging odors or taste. Four sizes ...8½" pie plate only.... **20¢**

THE TREND to oven meals makes a handy utility dish a necessity. It'll hold a good-sized rolled rib roast and potatoes and vegetables also! 10½" size **50¢**

DOUBLE GIFT! Use casserole for scalloped dishes or as a small roaster. Pie plate cover keeps food hot on table ... bakes delicious pies. 1 qt. size...... **50¢**

THESE FOUR NEW cups fill every household requirement. Quart liquid measure, pint liquid measure, one cup liquid measure and one cup dry measure. Give all four! Prices from... **15¢**

TRANSPARENT GLASS Flameware saucepan is new and smart...the latest thing! Wide flat bottom. Easy-pouring spout. And you can see the food cook! One quart size only...... **$1⁶⁵**

SHE'LL LOVE THIS! Sparkling clear Flameware double boiler cooks everything from creamy icings to perfect cereal. Smooth sides ...rounded corners. Washes clean in a jiffy. Quart size **$3⁴⁵**

EIGHT-PIECE Matched Set. There's 1½ quart casserole that does triple duty for baking, serving and storing. The cover is a perfect pie-plate or hot dish tile. Six 5-oz. matching custard cups can be used in the oven for puddings, custards and muffins and are wonderful for making and serving frozen desserts. In a good-looking gift box ...the most delightful surprise you'll ever find for as little as.............. **$1⁰⁰**

SMART IDEA! PLAN A PYREX WARE SHOWER

PYREX
OVENWARE
FLAMEWARE

AMAZING OFFER on stunning transparent Pyrex hot dish tile with your own initial! Measures 6¼" x 6¼". Holds steaming hot dishes. Has dozen other uses. For this regular 35¢ value, simply send 10¢ with your name and address to Corning Glass Works, Avery St., Corning, N. Y. Offer ends May 31, or when limited supply is exhausted.

HERE'S THE 17-piece Home Baker set, selected by home economists to meet 90% of all needs. Includes measuring cup, utility dish, loaf pan, pie plate, two cake dishes, four deep pie dishes, six custard cups and a wire rack. (Items can also be purchased separately.) Only **$2⁹⁵**

"PYREX" is a registered trade-mark of Corning Glass Works ... look for it for your own protection.

"Who says a bride can't cook?" This advertisement appeared in a 1941 publication. The items illustrated were available at your favorite department, five and ten, hardware, or grocery store. $3-$5 each.

87

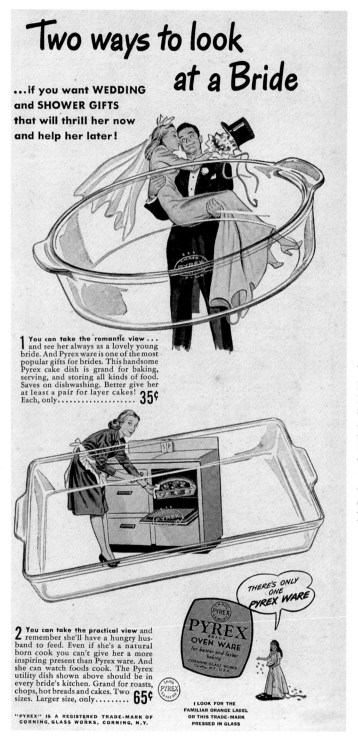

Two ways to look at a Bride

...if you want WEDDING and SHOWER GIFTS that will thrill her now and help her later!

1 You can take the romantic view . . . and see her always as a lovely young bride. And Pyrex ware is one of the most popular gifts for brides. This handsome Pyrex cake dish is grand for baking, serving, and storing all kinds of food. Saves on dishwashing. Better give her at least a pair for layer cakes! Each, only..................... **35¢**

2 You can take the practical view and remember she'll have a hungry husband to feed. Even if she's a natural born cook you can't give her a more inspiring present than Pyrex ware. And she can watch foods cook. The Pyrex utility dish shown above should be in every bride's kitchen. Grand for roasts, chops, hot breads and cakes. Two sizes. Larger size, only........ **65¢**

"PYREX" IS A REGISTERED TRADE-MARK OF CORNING GLASS WORKS, CORNING, N.Y.

THERE'S ONLY ONE PYREX WARE

PYREX BRAND OVEN WARE for better and faster baking CORNING GLASS WORKS Corning, N.Y. U.S.A.

I LOOK FOR THE FAMILIAR ORANGE LABEL OR THIS TRADE-MARK PRESSED IN GLASS

This advertisement promoting Pyrex as the perfect wedding and shower gift appeared in a June 1946 publication. The ad noted that "There's only one Pyrex Ware" and that " 'Pyrex' is a registered trade-mark of Corning Glass Works, Corning, N.Y." $3-$5 each.

Now...you can afford to use Fine Dinnerware at every meal

New **PYREX** ®
Dinnerware Combines Outstanding Strength and Beauty!

LOVELY NEW PYREX Dinnerware lets you treat your family like "special guests" every meal of the year— because this brand-new, modern dinnerware is as strong and durable as it is beautiful! Even the most constant use can't dim its smart looks, for its sparkling beauty goes *all the way through*, can't possibly wear off or grow dull! Enjoy the thrifty modern luxury of using exciting new PYREX Dinnerware at *your* house —bordered in your choice of four decorator colors!

16-Piece Service For Four, Only $6.95—With Color Borders Banded In 22-Carat Gold, $9.95

Here's proof of PYREX Dinnerware's amazing strength. The cups were used to hammer heavy 3-inch nails in laboratory tests.

Bread-and-Butter Plate, 50c
With Gold Band, 75c

Fruit-or-Sauce Dish, 50c
With Gold Band, 75c

Soup-or-Cereal Bowl, 60c
With Gold Band, 90c

Flamingo   Lime   Turquoise   Dove Gray

Announcing New Arrivals . . .
Three Beautiful Open-Stock Pieces
of PYREX Dinnerware!

Add these three brand-new beauties *(above left)* to your PYREX Dinnerware set for *extra* convenience . . . handy fruit-or-sauce dishes, soup-or-cereal bowls and bread-and-butter plates.

NEW PYREX Bakingware Dishes—To Match Or Harmonize With Your PYREX Dinnerware!

Other PYREX Bakingware Dishes in flamingo or lime include 8½" shallow dish, 60¢; 8¼" round dish, 95¢; 8" square dish, $1.25; 2-qt. covered bowl casserole, $1.50; 2-qt. oblong dish, $1.35. Packaged set, with all five dishes, $5.65; Casserole set, with covered bowl and 8¼" round dish (cover fits both), $2.45.

1½-qt. Deep Baking Dish $1.25   1½-qt. Oblong Dish $1.15

8-oz. Individual Casserole, 65c

There's only <u>one</u> **PYREX** ware, a product of 🌱 Corning Glass Works, Corning, N.Y.

"PYREX" is a registered trade-mark in the U. S. of Corning Glass Works, Corning, N. Y.

VISIT THE
CORNING GLASS
CENTER,
CORNING, N. Y.

This original Pyrex® advertisement appeared in the April, 1954 issue of *Family Circle*. The new Pyrex bakeware matched the new Pyrex dinnerware. *Advertisement Courtesy of Davis Collection.*

This original Pyrex® Gift Fair advertisement appeared in an issue of *Family Circle*, date unknown. Pyrex was available at leading stores. *Advertisement Courtesy of Davis Collection.*

This original Pyrex® insert came with a Pyrex 1-1/2 qt. utility dish. On the reverse of the insert is a selection of tested recipes. *Courtesy Davis Collection.* Original Insert $1-3.

Miscellaneous

Crystal glassware was always more effectively shown on glass shelving or black velvet material placed in front of mirrors. The sparkle of clear glass crystal could be emphasized by proper display. It had to be kept free from dust, dirt, and fingerprints. Frequent washing, dusting, and cleaning of the glassware were tasks required of salesgirls. Dusty glassware suggested that it had been on display for a long time and resulted in negative effects on sales.

Left: 1-3/16 oz. mustard jar with cover and crystal spoon. Right: 1/2 gallon cookie jar and cover. Mustard $30-$40. Cookie Jar $25-$30.

Left: 8 oz. baby sterilizer. Right: 8 oz. wide mouth nurser. $15-$20 each.

Left: 3" caster cup. Right: 3-3/4" coaster ash tray. Cup $1-$5. Tray $5-$10.

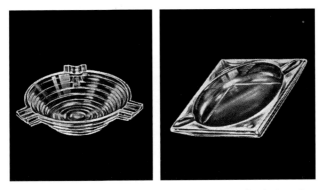

Left: 4" ash tray. Right: 3-1/2" square ash tray. $5-$10 each.

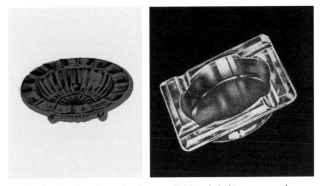

Left: 4" ruby footed ash tray. Right: 4-1/4" square ash tray. Ruby $20-$25. Square $5-$10.

Golden Iridescent Glassware

In 1943, this "Golden Iridescent Glassware" was offered for the first time at the same retail prices as similar plan glassware items. The decoration was fired on glass and would not wash off.

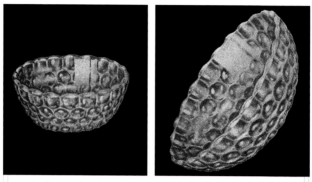

Left: 4-1/2" fruit or nappy. Right: 8-1/4" bowl. Fruit $25-$30. Bowl $40-$50.

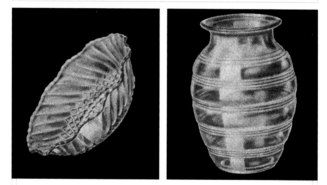

Left: 6" fancy crimped edge bonbon or nut dish. Right: 8" bulge shaped vase. Bonbon $25-$30. Vase $35-$40.

Left: 7-1/4" x 5-1/8" pear shaped candy jar with cover. Right: 5-7/8" x 5-1/8" apple shaped candy jar with cover. $40-$50 each.

Decorated Tumblers and
Ice Lip Jugs

Anchor Hocking "Hunting Scene" 9-1/2 oz. tall tumbler glassware, issued February 2, 1943. Available in red hunter, Chinese red hunter, and blue hunter. $10-$15 each.

Anchor Hocking "Litho-art Flowers" 9-1/2 oz. tall tumbler glassware. Available in red rose, yellow jonquil, Chinese red poppy, and blue iris. $10-$15 each.

Anchor Hocking "Litho-art Flowers" 13-1/2 oz. ice tea glassware. Available in red rose, yellow jonquil, Chinese red poppy, and blue iris. $15-$20 each.

Left: White jonquil 9-1/2 oz. tall tumbler. Right: 80 oz.
ice lipped "Red Rose" pitcher. Tumbler $10-$15.
Pitcher $20-$25.

Hand painted "Fruit" motif, 9-1/2 oz. tumblers. Available
in red, yellow, and blue. $10-$15 each.

"Animal Characters" 9-1/2 oz. tall tumblers. Available in red monkey, blue mule, Chinese red giraffe, and maroon camel. $20-$25 each.

"Dogwood" 9-1/2 oz. tall tumblers. Available in Chinese red, yellow, and green. $10-$15 each.

"Dogwood" 13-1/2 oz. tall tumblers. Available in Chinese red, yellow, and green. $10-$15 each.

Left: 80 oz. Chinese red ice lipped pitcher. Right: 80 oz. "Sail Boat" red pitcher. $25-$30 each.

"Sail Boat" 9-1/2 oz. tall tumblers. Available in red, yellow, and blue. $15-$20 each.

"Flower and Trellis" 9-1/2 oz. tall tumblers. Available in red, yellow, Chinese red, and turquoise blue. $10-$15 each.

"Flower and Trellis" 13-1/2 oz. tall tumblers. Available in red, yellow, Chinese red and turquoise blue. $10-$15 each.

Left: "Flower and Trellis" 80 oz. ice lipped pitcher. Right: 80 oz. ice lipped pitcher with red, hand painted flowers. $25-$30 each.

"Hand painted flowers" 9-1/2 oz. tall tumblers. Available in red, yellow, and blue. $10-$15 each.

"Hand painted flowers" 13-1/2 oz. tall tumblers. Available in red, yellow, and blue. $10-$15 each.

"Mexican Street Scene" 9-1/2 oz. tall tumblers. Available in red, yellow, and Chinese red. $20-$25 each.

"Mexican Street Scene" 13-1/2 oz. tall tumblers. Available in red, yellow, and Chinese red. $25-$30 each.

Left: "Mexican Garden and Street Scene" 80 oz. ice lipped pitcher. Right: "Mexican Garden" 80 oz. red ice lipped pitcher. $35-$40 each.

"Mexican Garden" 9-1/2 oz. tall tumblers. Available in red, yellow, and blue. $10-$15 each.

"Bird and Berries" 9-12/ oz. tall tumblers. Available with red bird and blue bird. $10-$15 each.

"Large Tulip" 9-1/2 oz. tall tumblers. Available in red, yellow, Chinese red, and turquoise. $10-$15 each.

"Large Tulip" 13-1/2 oz. tall tumblers. Available in red, yellow, Chinese red, and turquoise. $10-$15 each.

Left: "Large Tulip" 80 oz. red ice lipped pitcher. Right: "Spiral" 80 oz. Chinese red pitcher. $20-$25 each.

"Spiral" 9-1/2 oz. tall tumblers. Available in red,
Chinese red, yellow, and green. $10-$15 each.

"Spiral" 13-1/2 oz. tall tumblers. Available in red, Chinese
red, yellow, and green. $10-$15 each.

"Chinese Money" 9-1/2 oz. tall tumblers. Available in Chinese red, yellow, and blue. $10-$15 each.

"Rio Ribbon Bands" 5 oz. juice, 9-1/2 oz. tumbler, and 12 oz. ice tea. 5 oz. $5-$10. 9-1/2 oz. and 12 oz. $10-$15 each.

Left: "Rio Ribbon Bands" 80 oz. ice lipped pitcher. Right: "Carnival Stripe" 80 oz. ice lipped pitcher. $20-$25 each.

"Carnival Stripe" 6 oz. fruit juice, 9-1/2 oz. tumbler, and 13-1/2 oz. ice tea. 6 oz. $5-$10. 9-1/2 oz. and 13-1/2 oz. $10-$15 each.

"Colored and Gold Band" 11 oz. high ball. Available in red, yellow, green, and blue. $5-$10 each.

Left: 3-1/2 oz. decorated cocktail in red, white, and blue. Right: 3-1/2 oz. decorated cocktail in Chinese red, yellow, green, and orange. $2-$5 each.

Decorated 3-1/2 oz. cocktail in red bands, yellow bands, green bands, and blue bands. $2-$5 each.

Left: decorated 3-1/2 oz. gold cocktail. Right: "Gold Band" tumbler. Cocktail $2-$5. Tumbler $5-$10.

"Gold Band" 9 oz. tall
tumbler. $5-$10.

Left: "Betsy Ross" 9-1/2 oz. fancy tumbler. Right:
"Betsy Ross" 80 oz. ice lipped pitcher. Tumbler
$5-$10. Pitcher $15-$20.

"Garden Stripes" 5 oz. fancy fruit juice, 9-1/2 oz. fancy tumbler, and 12-1/2 oz. fancy ice tea. 5 oz. $5-$10. 9-1/2 oz. and 13-1/2 oz. $10-$15 each.

"Garden Stripes" 80 oz. ice lipped pitcher. $15-$20.

"Satin Tint" 9-1/2 oz. tumblers in rust, yellow, green, and blue. $5-$10 each.

Decorated 5 oz. tomato juice and orange juice glasses. $5-$10 each.

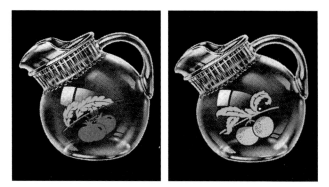

Decorated, 42 oz. tomato juice and orange juice
pitchers. $15-$20 each.

Decorated "Flower" in red, yellow, and green.
Davis Collection. $2-$4 each.

Artistic Cut Glass

It was wise for stores to establish a reputation as a place where a variety of glassware and gifts were available for purchase. The following glassware was issued January 12, 1943.

Laurel Genuine Cut Glass

Left: 5 oz. fancy fruit juice. Right: 6 oz. straight fruit juice. $10-$15 each.

Left: 11-1/2 oz. round bottom tumbler. Right: 1-1/2 oz. whiskey. $10-$15 each.

Left: 1 oz. sham whiskey. Right: 7-1/2 oz. old-fashioned glass and 3-1/2 oz. footed cocktail glass. $10-$15 each.

Left: 3-1/2 oz. stem cocktail glass and 3 oz. stem wine glass. Right: 6-1/2 oz. low stem sherbet and 8" salad plate. $10-$15 each.

Left: 6-3/4 oz. high stem sherbet and 10 oz. high stem goblet. Right: 80 oz. ice lipped ball pitcher. Sherbet/Goblet $10-$15 each. Pitcher $25-$30.

Checker Board Genuine Cut Glass

Left: 5 oz. fruit juice. Right: 10 oz. table tumbler. $10-$15 each.

Left: 6 oz. fruit juice. Right: 10 oz. high ball. $10-$15 each.

Left: 11-1/2 oz. round bottom tumbler. Right: 1 oz. sham whiskey. $10-$15 each.

Left: 7-1/2 oz. old fashioned and 3-1/2 oz. footed cocktail. Right: 3-1/2 oz. stem cocktail and 3 oz. stem wine. $10-$15 each.

Left: 6-1/2 oz. low stem sherbet with 6" sherbet plate. Right: 6-3/4 oz. high stem sherbet with 10 oz. high stem goblet. $10-$15 each.

Navajo Genuine Cut Glass

Left: 5 oz. fruit juice. Right: 10 oz. table tumbler.
$10-$15 each.

Left: 6 oz. fruit juice. Right: 10 oz. high ball. $10-$15 each.

Left:11-1/2 oz. round bottom tumbler. Right: 1 oz. whiskey. $10-$15 each.

Left: 7-1/2 oz. old fashioned with 3-1/2 oz. footed cocktail. Right: 3-1/2 oz. stem cocktail with 3 oz. stem wine. $10-$15 each.

Left: 6-1/2 oz. low stem sherbet with 6" sherbet plate. Right: 6-3/4 oz. high stem sherbet with 10 oz. high stem goblet. $10-$15 each.

Grape Genuine Cut Glass

Left: 3 oz. wine with 3-1/2 oz. cocktail. Right: 6-1/2 oz. low sherbet with 6" sherbet plate. $10-$15 each.

Left: 6-3/4 oz. high sherbet with 10 oz. goblet. Right: 3-1/2 oz. footed cocktail with 10 oz. tall tumbler. $10-$15 each.

Lily of the Valley Genuine Cut Glass

Left: 3-1/2 oz. stemmed cocktail glass with 3 oz. stemmed wine glass. Left: 6-1/2 oz. low stemmed sherbet. $10-$15.

Left: 6-3/4 oz. high stemmed sherbet with 10 oz. high stemmed goblet. Right: 7-1/2 oz. old-fashioned with 3-1/2 oz. footed cocktail. $10-$15 each.

Round bottom 11-1/2 oz. tall tumbler. $10-$15.

Wild Rose Genuine Cut Glass

Left: 10 oz. goblet. Right: 6-3/4 oz. high sherbet. $10-$15 each.

Left: 3 oz. wine. Right: 3-1/2 oz. cocktail. $10-$15 each.

Left: 5 oz. fruit juice. Right: 13 oz. high ball. $10-$15 each.

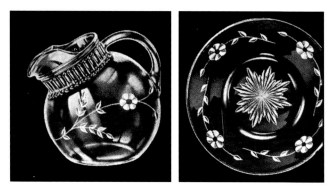

Left: 80 oz. ball jug. Right: 8" salad plate. Jug $25-$30.
Plate $10-$15.

Wild Rose refreshment set. Consists of 80 oz. jug and eight 9 oz. table tumblers. $105-$150 complete.

Floral Genuine Cut Glass

Left: 11-1/2 oz. high ball. Right: 8" salad plate. $10-$15 each.

Four sizes of crystal, drum-shaped globes, cut by hand with an appropriate design of water lilies and cattails. Customers recognized that these globes gave a decorative and interesting touch to their homes. Available in 1 quart, 2 quart, 1 gallon, and 2 gallon fish globes. $10-$15 each

Federal design 7" hurricane lamp. $10-$15.

Ivy bowl for ivy, roses, or goldfish. Available in 4" and 6". $10-$15 each.

Crystal Stemware

"Flower and Leaf Design" were fine quality, clear, thin-blown crystal in a tall graceful bell shape with a genuine cut design of small flowers and leaves. Issued May 26, 1942. No. 401: 9 oz. 8-1/4" high goblet. No. 402: 6 oz. 6" high saucer champagne. No. 403: 6 oz. 4-1/4" high stem sherbet. No. 404: 3 oz. 5-1/4" high cocktail glass. No. 405: 3 oz. 5-1/4" high wine glass. No. 406: 3 oz. 6-1/2" high claret. No. 408: 1 oz. 4-1/2" high cordial. No. 409: 12 oz. 5-1/2" high footed ice tea. No. 410: 9 oz. 5" high tumbler. No. 411: 5 oz. 4-1/4" high fruit juice glass. No. 413: 5 oz. 3-1/2" high oyster cocktail glass. No. 414: 4" diameter finger bowl. No. 416: 6" diameter sherbet plate. No. 417: 8" diameter salad plate. Prices for crystal stemware not provided due to significant geographical differences.

"Bubbles and Scroll Design" were tall, graceful bell shaped glassware with a genuine cut design of floral, bubbles, and scroll. Issued May 26: 1942. No. 421: 9 oz. 8-1/4" high goblet. No. 422: 6 oz. 6" high champagne. No. 423: 6 oz. 4-1/2" high stem sherbet. No. 424: 3 oz. 5-1/4" high cocktail. No. 425: 3 oz. 6-1/2" high wine glass. No. 426: 4 oz. 6-1/2" high claret glass. No. 428: 1 oz. 4-1/2" high cordial. No. 429: 12 oz. 5-1/2" high footed ice tea glass. No. 430: 9 oz. 5" high tumbler. No. 431: 5 oz. 4-1/2" high oyster cocktail. No. 434: 4-1/2" diameter finger bowl. No. 436: 6" diameter sherbet plate. No. 437: 8" diameter salad plate.

These tall, all-crystal fancy shaped pieces were cut with a "Floral Spray Design." No. 441: 9 oz. 7-1/2" high goblet. No. 442: 6 oz. 5-1/2" high champagne. No. 443: 6 oz. 4-3/4" high stem sherbet. No. 444: 3 oz. 5-1/4" high cocktail. No. 445: 3 oz. 5-3/4" high wine glass. No. 446: 4 oz. 6-1/4" high claret glass. No. 448: 1 oz. 4-1/8" high cordial. No. 449: 12 oz. 6-1/8" high footed ice tea. No. 450: 9 oz. 5-1/4" high tumbler. No. 451: 5 oz. 4-1/2" high fruit juice. No. 453: 5 oz. 3-1/2" high oyster cocktail. No. 454: 4-1/2" diameter finger bowl. No. 456: 6" diameter sherbet plate. No. 457: 8" diameter salad plate.

These were tall, flare shaped, all crystal etched and cut, large leaf design. No. 501: 9 oz. 7-1/2" high goblet. No. 502: 6 oz. 6-1/4" champagne. No. 503: 6 oz. 5-1/2" high stem sherbet. No. 504: 3 oz. 5-1/4" high cocktail. No. 505: 3 oz. 6" high wine glass. No. 506: 4 oz. 6-1/4" high claret glass. No. 508: 1 oz. 4-1/4" high cordial glass. No. 509: 12 oz. 6-1/2" high footed ice tea glass. No. 510: 9 oz. 5-3/4" tumbler. No. 511: 5 oz. 4-3/4" high fruit juice. No. 513: 5 oz. 3-1/2" high oyster cocktail. No. 514: 4-1/2" diameter finger bowl. No. 517: 8" diameter salad plate.

This egg shaped, plain crystal glassware was popular for hotels, restaurants and taverns. Issued May 26, 1942. No. 521: 9 oz. 7" high goblet. No. 522: 8 oz. 6" high goblet. No. 524: 6 oz. 6-1/4" high goblet. No. 525: 6 oz. 4-1/4" high saucer champagne. No. 526: 6 oz. 3-1/2" high sherbet. No. 528: 3 oz. 4-1/2" high cocktail. No. 529: 2-1/2 oz. 4-1/4" high cocktail. No. 530: 3 oz. 5" high wine glass. No. 531:1 oz. 3-1/4" high cordial glass. No. 533: 2 oz. 4-1/4" high wine glass. No. 534: 5 oz. 6" high tall champagne. No. 535: 9 oz. 4" high footed tumbler. No. 536: 5 oz. 3" high footed tumbler. No. 537: 3 oz. 2-1/2" high footed tumbler.

Plain, touraine shaped crystal for hotels, restaurants and taverns. No. 301: 9 oz. 6-1/2" high goblet. No. 302: 8 oz. 6-1/4" high goblet. No. 303: 7 oz. 6" high goblet. No. 304: 6 oz. 5-3/4" high goblet. No. 305: 6 oz. 4-1/2" high saucer champagne. No. 306: 6 oz. 3-1/2" high sherbet. No. 308: 3 oz. 4" high cocktail glass. No. 309: 2-1/2 oz. 3-7/8" high cocktail glass. No. 310: 3 oz. 4-3/4" high wine glass. No. 311: 1 oz. 3-3/4" high cordial glass. No. 312: 3/4 oz. 3-3/4" high pousse cafe glass.

134

Tall, concave shaped, genuine cut crystal in "Floral and Leaf Design," issued May 26, 1942. No. 321: 9 oz. 7-1/2" high goblet. No. 322: 6 oz. 5-5/8" high saucer champagne. No. 323: 6 oz. 4-1/2" high sherbet. No. 324: 3 oz. 5" high cocktail. No. 325: 3 oz. 6" high wine glass. No. 326: 4 oz. 5-7/8" high claret glass. No. 328: 1 oz. 4-1/8" high cordial. No. 329: 12 oz. 6-3/8" high ice tea. No. 330: 9 oz. 5-1/4" high tumbler. No. 331: 5 oz. 4-1/4" high fruit juice. No. 334: 4-1/2" diameter finger bowl. No. 336: 6" diameter sherbet plate. No 337: 8" diameter salad plate. No. 338: 5 oz. 3-1/2" high oyster cocktail.

Tall, bell shaped crystal glassware with large wild flower and leaf design. No. 341: 9 oz. 7-1/2" high goblet. No. 342: 6 oz. saucer champagne. No. 343: 6 oz. 4-3/8" high sherbet. No. 344: 3 oz. 5-1/8" high cocktail. No. 345: 3 oz. 6" high wine glass. No. 346: 4 oz. 5-3/4" high claret. No. 348: 1 oz. 4-1/2" high cordial. No. 349: 12 oz. 5-1/2" high ice tea. No. 350 9 oz. 5-1/4" high tumbler. No. 351: 5 oz. 4-3/8" fruit juice. No. 353: 5 oz. 3-1/2" high oyster cocktail. No. 354: 4-1/2" diameter finger bowl. No. 356: 6" diameter sherbet plate. No. 357: 8" diameter salad plate.

136

Tall, concave shaped, genuine cut all crystal lattice and leaf design, issued May 26, 1942. No. 361: 9 oz. 7-1/2" high goblet. No. 362: 6 oz. 5-5/8" high saucer champagne. No. 363: 6 oz. 4-1/2" high sherbet. No. 364: 3 oz. 5" high cocktail. No. 365: 3 oz. 6" high wine. No. 366: 4 oz. 5-7/8" high claret. No. 368: 1 oz. 4-1/8" high cordial. No. 369: 12 oz. 6-3/8" high ice tea. No. 370: 9 oz. 5-1/4" high tumbler. No. 371: 5 oz. 4-1/4" high fruit juice. No. 374: 4-1/2" diameter finger bowl. No 376: 6" diameter sherbet plate. No. 377: 8" diameter salad plate. No. 378: 5 oz. 3-1/2" high oyster cocktail.

Tall, bell shaped glassware. No. 381: 9 oz. 7-1/2" high goblet. No. 382: 6 oz. 5-3/4" high saucer champagne. No. 383: 6 oz. 4-3/8" cocktail glass. No. 385: 3 oz. 6" high wine glass. No. 386: 4 oz. 5-3/4" high claret. No. 388: 1 oz. 4-1/2" high claret. No. 389: 12 oz. 5-1/2" high ice tea. No. 390: 9 oz. 5-1/4" high tumbler. No. 391: 5 oz. 4-3/8" high fruit juice. No. 393: 5 oz. 3-1/2" high oyster cocktail. No. 394: 4-1/2" diameter finger bowl. No. 396: 6" diameter sherbet plate. No. 397: 8" diameter salad plate.

Indiana Glassware

Hand made glassware from the Indiana Glass Company, Dunkirk, Indiana (1907-present), was finished in the tradition of "Early American" craftsmanship but styled to meet modern demands. The extraordinary values shown here could be found in leading department stores throughout the country. All pieces were highly polished, reflecting a sparkling brilliancy usually found in glassware selling at several times this price. Each piece has a gold label reading "Indiana Made in U.S.A." Issued June 2, 1942.

Brilliant, sparkling mirror glass crystal with deep reflecting prismatic designs included a pair of twin, 5-1/2" high candlesticks; a footed, 14" diameter snack or sandwich tray; three piece sugar and cream with 10-3/4" tray; 11-1/4" x 7-1/4" oblong console bowl; covered 6-1/2" diameter candy box; and footed 13" diameter fruit bowl. Candlesticks $35-$40 pair. Snack Tray $50-$60. Sugar/Cream $25-$30 pair. Tray $20-$25. Console Bowl $25-$30. Candy Box $40-$50. Fruit Bowl $30-$35.

An early American colonial highly pressed pattern with deep impressed intaglio etched grape design on each piece. Included a pair of 5-1/4" high twin candlesticks; 13-1/4" diameter snack or sandwich tray; three partition, 14-1/4" x 6-1/2" relish dish; 13-1/4" diameter console bowl; three-toed, 5-1/4" high, 7-1/2" diameter flower bowl; and a deep 10-1/2" diameter fruit bowl. Candlesticks $50-$60 pair. Snack Tray $60-$65. Relish Dish $25-$30. Console Bowl $30-$35. Flower Bowl $60-$65. Fruit Bowl. $45-$50.

Deeply impressed, highly polished magnolia leaf design. Included a footed 13-1/2" diameter snack or sandwich tray; covered 7-1/4" high, 6-1/2" diameter footed candy bowl with cover; footed, vase-shaped 4" high candlesticks; 3" high sugar bowl, 3-3/4" high cream pitcher, and 10-1/2" long tray; footed 11" diameter deep fruit bowl; and footed 12-1/2" diameter console bowl. Snack Tray $60-$70. Candy Bowl $65-$70. Candlesticks $70-$80 pair. Sugar/Creamer $35-$40. Tray $25-$30. Fruit Bowl $75-$80. Console Bowl $75-$80.

Large handled 10-1/2" high x 12" basket. $80-$100. This rich, attractive, fruit orchard decorated glassware (shown in this and the next two pictures) is a heavy pressed full finished crystal. The fruit design is raised or embossed, hand painted in transparent natural colors. All pieces are footed and were excellent for large buffet or table pieces. They could be used separately or combined with other pieces to provide a beautiful centerpiece for the table.

Console set consisted of a deep 12" x 8-1/4" bowl and a pair of 5-1/2" high twin candlesticks. $100-$150 complete.

Footed table pieces included a 13-1/2" diameter snack or sandwich tray, a 12" console bowl, and a 11-1/4" diameter deep fruit bowl. $50-$65 each.

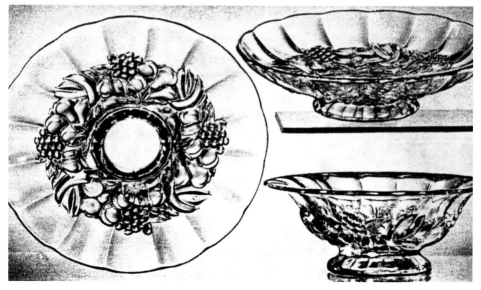

THE MARION GLASS MANUFACTURING CO.
MARION, OHIO

S. S. KRESGE CO.

Store No.

Our Order No.
Customer's Order
Invoice Date
Invoice Number

SHIPPED VIA

TERMS: 1% 15 days—Net 30 Days

Number of Packages	Kind of Packages	Dozens in Each Package	DESCRIPTION		Total Quantity	Price Per Dozen	TOTAL
			1½ oz. Straight Whiskey 2½ oz. Bell Whiskey 8 oz. Bell 9 oz. Barrel, plain 9 oz. Standard	Cut 508 Tumblers			
			9 oz. Goblet 5 oz. Sherbet 5 oz. Saucer Champagne 3 oz. Wine 9 oz. Standard Tumbler	Princess Bell Shape Optic Cut 520			
			#50-10" Crimp Top #4 -10" Crimp Top #8 -10" Plain Top #1288-10" Plain Top	Special Vases Crystal			
			Goblet Saucer Champagne Sherbet Cocktail 5 oz. Flared Tumbler 9 oz. Flared Tumbler 10 oz. Tall Flared Tumbler	Pink Ware Cut 520			
			#50 Bud Vase #8 Bud Vase #1288 Bud Vase #4 Bud Vase	Special Vases Pink			
			Cut 508 Tumblers			.34	
			Princess Bell Shape			1.85	
			9 oz. Tumbler Cut 520			.55	
			Special Vases, Crystal			1.85	
			Pink Stemware Cut 520			1.90	
			Pink Flared Tumblers			.75	
			Special Vases, Pink			1.90	

This original glassware invoice for the S.S. Kresge Co. was issued by The Marion Glass Manufacturing Co., Marion, Ohio. *Davis Collection*. Invoice $20-$25.

Index